Pony Express!

WANTED

YOUNG SKINNY WIRY FELLOWS
not over eighteen. Must be expert
riders willing to risk death daily.
Orphans preferred. WAGES $25 per
week. Apply, *Central Overland Express, Alta Bldg., Montgomery St.*

For Dianne Hess
— *S.K.*

For Jim, a true pard
— *D.A.*

For her special help and thoughtfulness, I would like to thank Paula E. Rabkin,
Research Associate, Postal History, the United States Postal Service, Washington,
D.C. I would also like to thank Gary Chilcote, Museum Director,
Patee House Museum, St. Joseph, Missouri.

Photo Credits:
Photo credit for pictures 3 through 8:
courtesy of the United States Postal Service.

Photo 2 courtesy of the National Postal Museum, Smithsonian Institution.

Library of Congress Cataloging-in-Publication Data

Kroll, Steven.
Pony express!/Steven Kroll; illustrated by Dan Andreasen.
p. cm.
Includes bibliographical references and index.
Summary: Discusses the eighteen month history, officially
beginning April 3, 1860, of the mail delivery between Saint Joseph,
Missouri, and Sacramento, California, known as the Pony Express.
ISBN 0-590-20239-1
1. Pony express—History—Juvenile literature. 2. Postal service—
United States—History—Juvenile literature. [1. Pony express.]
I. Andreasen, Dan, ill. II. Title.
HE6375.P65K76 1996
383´.143´0973—dc20   95-10853
CIP
AC

12 11 10 9 8 7 6 5 4 3 2 1   6 7 8 9/9 0 1/0
Printed in the U.S.A.
First printing, March 1996

Because the term "Indians" was commonly used to describe Native Americans in
the nineteenth century, I have used that term in this book.

The illustrations in this book were done in oil paint
on Gesso primed board.
Map by Heather Saunders
Designed by David Turner

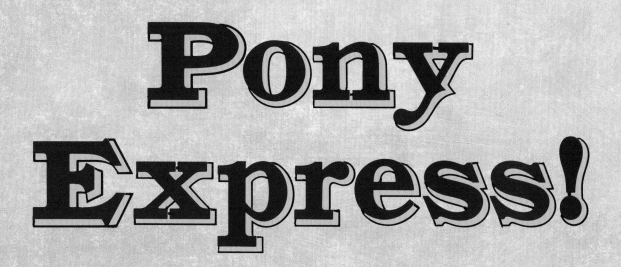

Pony Express!

by

STEVEN KROLL

illustrated by

DAN ANDREASEN

SCHOLASTIC
HARDCOVER

SCHOLASTIC INC.

New York

Before

On January 24, 1848, gold was discovered at Sutter's Mill in the Sacramento Valley. Within two years, nearly 300,000 people had rushed to California to seek their fortunes. Far from home, they wanted news, and they wanted mail.

Before the Gold Rush, mail to California went by ship around Cape Horn at the tip of South America. It could take six months to arrive. As of January 1, 1849, the U.S. Government arranged with the Pacific Mail Steamship Company to provide monthly service between New York and San Francisco. To do this, ships traveled up and down both coasts, while mules and eventually a railroad took the mail across the Isthmus of Panama. Delivery time: a little more than three weeks with luck.

But the people of California wanted better, faster service. Cross-country mule teams and four-horse coaches were tried and defeated by Indian raids and terrible winter weather. Congress even bought camels, but they were used to the soft sand of the Sahara Desert. Their feet got sore on the rocky trails of the Far West.

In 1856, 75,000 Californians signed a petition to Congress demanding a route overland by stagecoach. In 1857, the Post Office Department accepted a bid from John Butterfield, a New York stagecoach operator.

The North and South were on the brink of civil war. Each side wanted the mail route in their section of the country. Aaron Brown, the U.S. Postmaster General, was from Tennessee. He chose the southern route.

The route was known as the Oxbow. It had an advantage over the Central Route, or Overland Trail, followed by so many gold seekers. It avoided the subzero temperatures of the Great Plains and the dangerous passes of the Sierra Nevada Mountains. The disadvantage was that it was 760 miles longer, and wide open to attack by Indians, angry at the invasion of their land.

For better or for worse, the Butterfield Overland Mail couldn't deliver in less than twenty-three days. That wasn't fast enough, especially after silver and gold were discovered in Colorado and Nevada toward the end of 1858. More people wanted mail sooner!

Russell, Majors, and Waddell of Leavenworth, Kansas, was one of the largest freighting companies supplying the West. In 1858, the impulsive William H. Russell had talked his partners into lending him money for a stagecoach line between Leavenworth and Denver, Colorado, that failed. To help pay their bills, the partners bought a firm with the mail contract between St. Joseph, Missouri, and Salt Lake City, Utah. They moved the Denver stages onto the Central Route and built new stations.

With mail on his mind, Russell had several conversations with Senator William M. Gwin of California over the winter of 1859–1860. He left Washington, D.C., committed to starting a "horse express" — ten days from St.

Joseph, Missouri, to Sacramento, California — and to starting it in two months' time at his company's expense!

There would be a chain of riders relaying the mail from one station to the next. Galloping west from St. Joseph and east from Sacramento, one rider in each direction would set off the chain. Each would cover an average of seventy-five miles between "home" stations and change horses at least seven times at relay stations along the way. Finishing his stint, a rider would hand the mail to the next rider in the chain. Then he'd rest, wait for that same rider to bring the mail coming the other way, and gallop back to the station he'd started from. All the while, the mail would move swiftly back and forth across the country.

Alexander Majors thought the plan would lose money.

"If you won't join me, I'll go it alone," Russell said.

"All right," said Majors, "we're in."

They already had the stations to Salt Lake, but they were too far apart. More had to be located, built, and equipped, and from Salt Lake to Sacramento, they had to start from scratch.

Where there was timber, stations were built of logs. Farther west, in barren Nevada and Utah, they were made of adobe or rock. Sometimes they were just caves hollowed out of hillsides.

There would be 190 stations in five divisions, more than 400 station hands, and close to 500 horses. The horses had to be the best: sleek, fast thoroughbreds for the flat Great Plains, tough, sturdy mustangs for the mountains and deserts of the West.

Their riders had to be fit and weigh less than 125 pounds. Eighty had to be hired for the 1,966-mile route. Twenty was the preferred age, but many were under eighteen.

Those who made it had to sign a pledge: no swearing, no drinking, no quarreling. Alexander Majors gave each one a small leatherbound Bible.

On April 3, 1860, with many stations still unfinished, "the Pony" was ready to go.

The First Ride
April 3 – April 13, 1860

It was late. Leading his bay mare, Johnson William "Bill" Richardson paced back and forth in front of the Patee House, the fine new hotel in St. Joseph, Missouri. The dark, wiry twenty-three-year-old had been chosen by lot to make the historic first run of the Pony Express.

A crowd had gathered. Flags were flying. A brass band played. But the time was after 5:00 P.M. Where was the mail? It should have arrived half an hour ago.

Russell and Majors had set up offices at the Patee House. They were there for the celebration but only a little concerned. A message had arrived by telegraph. The special mail carrier from Washington had missed a rail connection in Detroit. He'd reached Palmyra Junction, Missouri, three hours behind schedule.

Majors and Mayor M. Jeff Thompson gave speeches about progress and how the railroad would soon replace the Pony Express. The restless crowd began plucking hairs from the pony's mane and tail as souvenirs. A cannon on a nearby hilltop boomed. With the crowd following him in a kind of parade, Richardson rode off to the post office.

Meanwhile, Addison Clark, the best engineer on the Hannibal and St. Joseph line, was on his way. His locomotive was the wood-burning *Missouri*. Hitched to its tender was a specially constructed mail car with built-in seats for railway officials.

Top speed for a freight train at that time was about fifteen miles per hour. The roadbeds were loose, the light rails easily thrown out of line. The first fifty miles out of Palmyra Junction were level and straight. Clark did them at sixty, and he never let up.

At Macon he had to stop for fuel. As the train screeched to a halt, men on a high platform dumped armloads of wood into the storage bins. The stop lasted only fifteen seconds.

Out of Macon, there was rough country and a lot of twists and turns. It was a wild ride for the passengers, but when Clark pulled into St. Jo at 6:30 P.M., he had set a record that would last for fifty years: 206 miles in four hours and fifty-one minutes. He'd also picked up half an hour on the schedule.

At the post office, Richardson was waiting. The postmaster brought the *mochila* with the mail.

The *mochila* was a leather covering that fit over the small, light saddle with a hole for the horn in front and a slit for the cantle behind. At the corners were four locked leather boxes called *cantinas*. In them were forty-nine letters, five private telegrams, a special edition of the *St. Joseph Gazette,* other newspapers, and a telegram of congratulations from President Buchanan. All were on tissue-thin paper and wrapped in oiled silk for protection. The cost was three dollars a half ounce to Salt Lake City and five dollars all the way to Sacramento.

Richardson carried a horn, a rifle, and two Colt revolvers, though later riders carried only a single revolver to reduce the weight. At 7:15 P.M., he took off for the foot of Francis Street and the ferry across the Missouri River.

At Troy, Kansas he changed horses, flipping the *mochila* from one saddle to the other. He was allowed two minutes, but he did it in seconds. Then on through Cold Spring, Kennekuk, and Kickapoo, changing horses at each. At 11:30 P.M., he roared into Granada, shaving forty-five minutes off the lost time.

Don Rising, not yet seventeen, was ready. He transferred the *mochila* and was off into the darkness through Log Chain, Seneca, and Guittard's Station to Marysville at dawn. There everyone was awake and cheering as Jack Keetley took over and headed for the Big Blue River, the prairies beyond, and Henry Wallace, the next rider, in Hollenberg.

Rider followed rider along the settlers' Trail of Scars. When the sun came up on April 9, the mail was at Salt Lake City, halfway there.

Back on April 3, as the Pony Express was getting underway in St. Joseph, another opening day celebration was taking place in San Francisco. Decked out in miniature American flags, a yellow pony pranced in front of the Alta Telegraph Office. The *mochila,* jammed with eighty-five letters, bore the words *Overland Pony Express.*

Just before 4:00 P.M., James Randall mounted up. In his excitement, he mounted from the wrong side (the right). Then, with the crowd cheering, he headed for the waterfront and the stern-wheeler *Antelope.*

That was as far as he would ride. For opening day, San Francisco wanted a show. From then on, there would be no fanfare as mail was delivered to a steamship and taken upriver to Sacramento. There the eastbound Pony Express really began.

The *Antelope* didn't reach Sacramento until after two in the morning. By then it was raining hard.

Billy Hamilton was at the dock. The express agent grabbed the *mochila,* inserted the local mail, and flung it on the pony's back. Hamilton was off into the soggy night with no one to wish him well. He rode hard, knowing that rain in the valley meant snow in the mountains for the next rider. He wanted to give that rider extra time.

He passed Fort Sutter and went up the American River. At Folsom, he got a fresh horse and sped on to do the same at Five Mile House, Fifteen Mile House, Mormon Tavern, and Placerville. When he pulled into Sportsman's Hall, he'd beaten the schedule by half an hour.

Warren Upson, son of the editor of the *Sacramento Union*, was next. A great rider, great shot, and "weatherproof," he chose a stocky, trailwise pony for the difficult trail ahead, the most grueling stint on the entire route. As he started for Strawberry Station, it was snowing. The wind blew the snow into his face. More often than not, he had to dismount and lead his pony.

Blinded by snow and wind, he kept heading upward, winding up the slopes of the Sierra Nevadas. Only when he felt himself going down did he know he'd crossed the summit of a pass.

Strawberry was snowed in, but Upson changed horses and slogged on through to Hope Valley and Woodbridge. From there to Genoa and his home station of Carson City, Nevada, conditions got better. He handed the *mochila* to his relief rider, "Pony Bob" Haslam.

Between Carson City and Salt Lake City was a wasteland thick with alkali dust. There were forty-seven lonely stations, each one little more than a place to change horses. But Pony Bob had courage and spirit. He galloped on to Buckland's Station.

And on they went — to Ruby Valley and Egan Canyon, to Deep Creek, Utah, and Camp Floyd. East of Salt Lake City, sometime on April 8, the east and westbound riders crossed. No one knows if they even waved their hats.

Heading east through the Rocky Mountains, the Wyoming wilderness loomed, followed by the Continental Divide, Devil's Gate, and the foaming Sweetwater River. The rider made a stop at Fort Laramie, then went on to Chimney Rock, Nebraska.

Outside Julesburg, the Platte River was flooded. Horse and rider plunged in, but the horse lost its footing and was hurled downstream. The rider saved the *mochila* and reached the opposite bank. A spectator gave him another horse. Someone else went after the one in the river.

After Fort Kearney, there were grassy plains. When Bill Richardson rode back off the ferry in St. Joseph, Missouri, and delivered the eastbound mail to the Pony Express office at the Patee House, it was 3:55 P.M. on April 13.

Crowds cheered. There were fireworks and bonfires. The cannon boomed again. Ten days across the continent! The Pony Express had done it.

In California the same was true.

Warren Upson got the westbound *mochila* on April 12 at 3:30 P.M. in Carson City. He headed back over the Sierras. The storm was over, but now freight wagons and mule trains blocked the way. They were bringing supplies to the Carson Valley mines. Upson struggled on, frequently leaving the trail and stumbling through snowdrifts. He arrived at Sportsman's Hall in California at 1:00 P.M. on April 13.

Billy Hamilton took the mail into Sacramento. When he arrived on the Fort Sutter Road around 5:25 P.M., a welcoming committee galloped up. As they turned sharply to lead him back to town, the dust from their horses' hooves left him choking.

In town, J Street was lined with people. Women stood on balconies. Men and boys clambered onto rooftops.

A horseman appeared carrying a small flag. More horsemen with flags followed. Cannons were fired. Everyone shouted and waved hats and handkerchiefs. Finally Hamilton arrived, trotted up to the agency office, and delivered the mail on time!

But then he was off on the *Antelope* for San Francisco. Arriving at 11:30 P.M. to bonfires and rockets, he was swept into a parade. A band played "See, the Conquering Hero Comes." Fire companies marched. A woman rushed forward and tied her bonnet on the pony's head. When they reached the Alta Telegraph Office, it was lit up with candles. The Pony Express was a triumph.

After

For a month "the Pony" was right on schedule. Then the
Paiute Indians began attacking settlers and destroying stations
around Carson City. The route became unsafe for 250 miles.

The Paiutes had been through a terrible winter. They blamed
the prospectors for destroying their timber and ignoring them.
Skirmishes went on for weeks and turned into a war that
lasted another month. During that month, the Pony Express
didn't move.

Afterward, William Russell not only restored service, he
doubled it to twice a week. At that exhausting pace, not many
riders lasted a full year, but while they rode, they beat the
weather, Indian attacks, and loneliness. When a rider reached
the end of a run and found no relief, he galloped on and did
another stint.

Only one *mochila* was ever lost, but without a government contract, Russell, Majors, and Waddell kept losing money. When Russell couldn't win Congress over in the fall of 1860, he made a very questionable deal. He "borrowed" thousands of dollars in bonds from the Indian Trust Fund.

On December 24, Russell was arrested and thrown in jail. He was released on bail and never brought to trial, but around this time Congress was debating a new mail contract. Russell's disgrace didn't help his cause.

By February 1861, the Civil War was near. With Southern sympathizers raiding John Butterfield's stations, he was told to move his coaches to the Central Route. The Pony Express was merged with Butterfield-Wells Fargo under the name Overland Mail Company. On March 2, the company received a million-dollar-a-year contract to continue carrying the mail six days a week by coach and by Pony Express "until the completion of the transcontinental telegraph."

The telegraph sent messages across a wire by electrical impulse. Before 1849, it had reached Missouri. Even California had a system connecting the cities with the goldfields. Just before the Pony Express began, Edward Creighton traveled the Central Route by mule, confirming that it was possible to set telegraph poles coast to coast.

In June 1860, Congress passed a bill offering $40,000 a year for ten years to any company that could connect the telegraph lines, east to west. That September, Hiram Sibley, president of Western Union, got the contract. Two new companies were formed to string the wire: the Overland Telegraph Company between Omaha and Salt Lake City, and the Pacific Telegraph Company between Salt Lake and Virginia City.

War began in April 1861. People wanted more news faster. By July, work on the transcontinental telegraph was underway.

Pony riders were helpful and kept carrying mail between the terminals, but the closer those terminals got to one another, the shorter the rides became. On October 24, the two telegraph lines were completed. On October 26, the Pony Express closed down after only eighteen months.

There would be many more improvements in mail service, from the transcontinental railroad to the airplane and the computer, but no one would ever forget those brave boys on their bold ponies.

AUTHOR'S NOTE

In early America, there was more mail to and from England than there was between the colonies. People carried messages on foot and on horseback, but to handle the overseas mail, Richard Fairbanks' tavern in Boston became the first mail drop post office in America in 1639.

Post routes, post roads, post riders, postmasters general, and more post offices followed. By 1800, the Post Office Department was operating stagecoaches on the better post roads, and a little more than ten years later, steamboats were carrying mail to towns that could only be reached by water. The railroads got their first mail contract in 1836.

In the early nineteenth century, no one used envelopes. A letter was a folded sheet with the address written on the outside. Postage stamps appeared in 1847, but up until 1855, the sender could ask the recipient to pay the postage. Mailing or receiving a letter meant going to the post office until city delivery and city street mail collection boxes appeared in the early 1860s. Rural free delivery would have to wait for the beginning of the twentieth century.

Many people in St. Joseph, Missouri, believe that a colorful character named Johnny Fry was the first Pony Express rider out of the Patee House on April 3, 1860. Most others seem to agree that it was Bill Richardson.

William F. "Buffalo Bill" Cody was the youngest rider at fifteen. His route was between Red Buttes and Three Crossings, but he wasn't among the first and left after only a few months.

Samuel F. B. Morse's telegraph, in use since 1844, was made up of a transmitter and a receiver joined by a wire that carried electric current from a battery. The transmitter operator pressed a key that connected and broke a circuit. The resulting short and long impulses made up the dots and dashes of Morse code. The receiver contained a steel stylus that passed over a groove and recorded the dots and dashes so they could be interpreted.

Although the telegraph made the Pony Express unnecessary, the completion of the transcontinental railroad in 1869 made it possible to move more mail faster. Rail service continued to grow until 1930, but by 1920, airmail across the continent was a reality. By 1970, trains were no longer carrying first-class mail.

At the beginning of the twentieth century, mail was still sorted by the pigeonhole method that dated back to colonial times. By the 1950s, new machines had been introduced that sorted, canceled, and coded and read addresses automatically. By the 1960s, however, the volume of business mail, made possible by the computer, had become overwhelming.

To help, the ZIP Code (Zone Improvement Plan) was developed, then followed, in 1983, by the ZIP + 4 Code, which added a hyphen and four digits to the five-digit ZIP Code. Today multiline optical character readers (MLOCRs) can read a printed address, spray a bar code on an envelope, then sort more than nine of those envelopes a second. For handwritten script mail or mail that cannot be read by OCRs, the remote bar-coding system (RBCS) provides bar coding.

More than 160 billion pieces of mail are delivered every year in the United States. There are 40,000 post offices and more than 720,000 postal employees. And now we have fax machines, Express Mail, numerous private overnight delivery services, and E-mail. The riders of the Pony Express would hardly believe their eyes!

Pony Express Route

*Map does not include every station

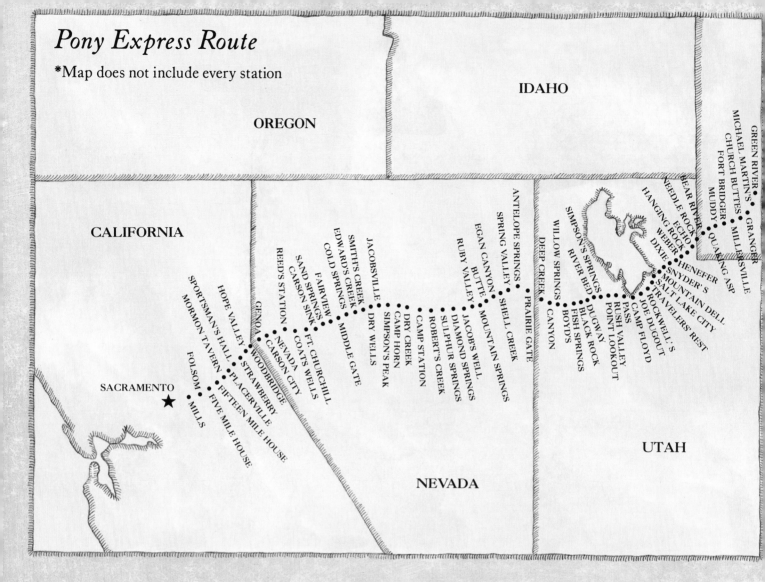

OREGON

IDAHO

CALIFORNIA

NEVADA

UTAH

★ SACRAMENTO

MILLS
FOLSOM
FIFTEEN MILE HOUSE
FIVE MILE HOUSE
PLACERVILLE
MORMON TAVERN
STRAWBERRY
SPORTSMAN'S HALL
WOODBRIDGE
HOPE VALLEY
GENOA
CARSON CITY
NEVADA
REED'S STATION
COATS WELLS
CARSON SINK
SAND SPRINGS
FT. CHURCHILL
FAIRVIEW
COLD SPRINGS
EDWARD'S CREEK
MIDDLE GATE
SMITH'S CREEK
JACOBSVILLE
DRY WELLS
SIMPSON'S PEAK
CAMP HORN
DRY CREEK
CAMP STATION
ROBERT'S CREEK
SULPHUR SPRINGS
DIAMOND SPRINGS
JACOB'S WELL
MOUNTAIN SPRINGS
BUTTE
RUBY VALLEY
EGAN CANYON
SHELL CREEK
SPRING VALLEY
ANTELOPE SPRINGS
PRAIRIE GATE
DEEP CREEK
WILLOW SPRINGS
CANYON
BOYD'S
SIMPSON'S SPRINGS
RIVER BED
FISH SPRINGS
BLACK ROCK
DUGWAY
POINT LOOKOUT
RUSH VALLEY
PASS
CAMP FLOYD
JOE DUGOUT
ROCKWELL'S
TRAVELERS' REST
SALT LAKE CITY
MOUNTAIN DELL
SNYDER'S
DIXIE
WEBBER
HENEFER
HANGING ROCK
ECHO
NEEDLE ROCK
BEAR RIVER
QUAKING ASP
MUDDY
FORT BRIDGER
CHURCH BUTTES
MICHAEL MARTIN'S
MILLERSVILLE
GRANGER
GREEN RIVER

Mini Photo Museum

1. When the Gold Rush began, clipper ships were introduced to move cargo, including mail, faster. The Flying Cloud (above) set a speed record for clippers in 1851, sailing from New York to San Francisco in 89 days.

2. The Spearfish Coach, Deadwood, South Dakota, delivering mail around the mid-1850s.

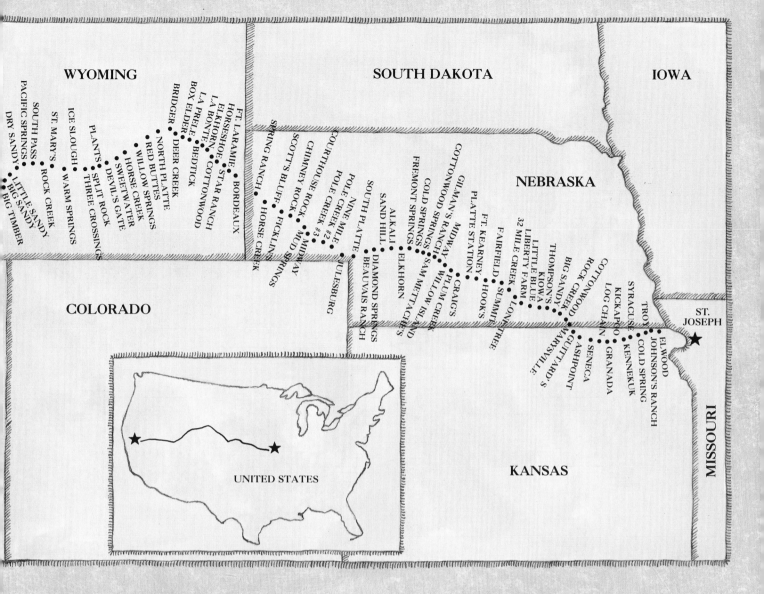

WYOMING

SOUTH DAKOTA

IOWA

NEBRASKA

COLORADO

KANSAS

MISSOURI

ST. JOSEPH

UNITED STATES

DRY SANDY
BIG SANDY
LITTLE SANDY
PACIFIC SPRINGS
SOUTH PASS
ST. MARY'S
ROCK CREEK
ICE SLOUGH
WARM SPRINGS
THREE CROSSINGS
SPLIT ROCK
PLANTS
DEVIL'S GATE
SWEETWATER
HORSE CREEK
WILLOW SPRINGS
RED BUTTES
NORTH PLATTE
DEER CREEK
BRIDGER
BOX ELDER
LA PRELE
BEDTICK
LA BONTE
COTTONWOOD
ELKHORN
STAR RANCH
HORSESHOE
FT. LARAMIE
BORDEAUX

SPRING RANCH
SCOTT'S BLUFF
FICKLINS
HORSE CREEK
CHIMNEY ROCK
MUD SPRINGS
MIDWAY
COURTHOUSE ROCK
POLE CREEK #3
POLE CREEK #2
NINE MILE
JULESBURG
POLE CREEK
SOUTH PLATTE
ALKALI
SAND HILL
DIAMOND SPRINGS
BEAUVAIS RANCH
ELKHORN

GILMAN'S RANCH
COTTONWOOD SPRINGS
COLD SPRINGS
FREMONT SPRINGS
MIDWAY
CRAIG'S
WILLOW CREEK
PLUM CREEK
SAM MCTAGHE'S
WILLOW ISLAND
PLATTE STATION
FT. KEARNEY
HOOK'S
FAIRFIELD
SUMMIT
32 MILE
LONE TREE
LIBERTY FARM
LITTLE BLUE
KIOWA
THOMPSON'S
BIG SANDY
MILLERSVILLE
GUTTARD'S
MARYSVILLE
ASHPOINT
COTTONWOOD
ROCK CREEK
LOG CHAIN
GRANADA
SENECA
KICKAPOO
KENNEKUK
SYRACUSE
COLD SPRING
TROY
JOHNSON'S RANCH
ELWOOD

3. Lehigh Valley Railroad, United States Mail Railway Post Office car, unloading mail around 1913.

4. Street letter collection, with truck, around 1913.

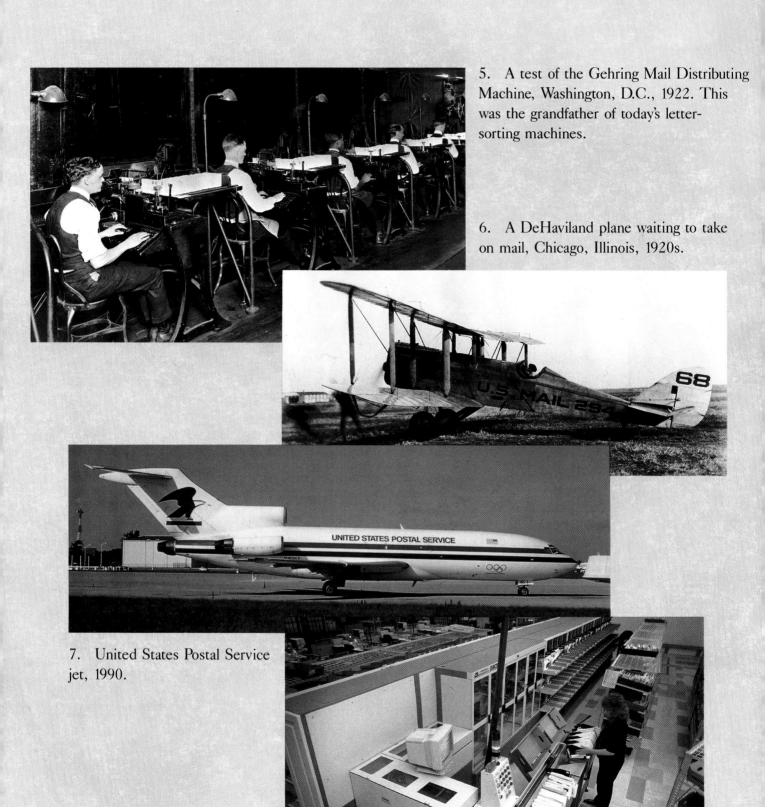

5. A test of the Gehring Mail Distributing Machine, Washington, D.C., 1922. This was the grandfather of today's letter-sorting machines.

6. A DeHaviland plane waiting to take on mail, Chicago, Illinois, 1920s.

7. United States Postal Service jet, 1990.

8. Delivery bar code sorter, Long Island, NY, 1992.

BIBLIOGRAPHY

Adams, Samuel Hopkins, *The Pony Express*. Illustrated by Lee J. Ames. New York: Random House, 1950.

Bradley, Glenn D., *The Story of the Pony Express*. Chicago: A. C. McClurg & Company, 1913.

Chapman, Arthur, *The Pony Express: The Record of a Romantic Adventure in Business*. New York and Chicago: A. L. Burt Company, 1932.

Driggs, Howard R., *The Pony Express Goes Through: An American Saga Told by Its Heroes*. Illustrated by William H. Jackson. New York: Frederick A. Stokes & Co., 1935.

Hulbert, Archer Butler, *Forty-niners: The Chronicle of the California Trail*. Boston: Little, Brown and Company, 1931.

Jackson, Joseph Henry, editor, *Gold Rush Album*. New York: Charles Scribner's Sons, 1949.

Logan, Sheridan A., *Old Saint Jo, Gateway to the West, 1799–1932*. Illustrated by John Falter. St. Joseph, Missouri: John Sublett Logan Foundation, 1979.

Russell, Don, *The Lives and Legends of Buffalo Bill*. Norman, Oklahoma: University of Oklahoma Press, 1960.

Sell, Henry Blackman, and Victor Weybright, *Buffalo Bill and the Wild West*. New York: Oxford University Press, 1955.

Thompson, Robert Luther, *Wiring a Continent: The History of the Telegraph Industry in the United States, 1832–1866*. Princeton, New Jersey: Princeton University Press, 1947.

United States Postal Service, *History of the United States Postal Service, 1775–1993*. Washington, D.C.: United States Postal Service, 1993.

van der Linde, Laurel, *The Pony Express*. New York: New Discovery Books, Maxwell Macmillan International, 1993.

Visscher, William Lightfoot, *A Thrilling and Truthful History of the Pony Express*. Skokie, Illinois: Rand McNally, 1908.

West, Tom, *Heroes on Horseback: The Story of the Pony Express*. New York: Four Winds Press, 1969.

INDEX